LOVE

AN ANTHOLOGY

LOVE

AN ANTHOLOGY

an enchanting collection of art,
verse and prose

LORENZ BOOKS

This edition is published by Lorenz Books,
an imprint of Anness Publishing Ltd,
Blaby Road, Wigston,
Leicestershire LE18 4SE;
info@anness.com

www.lorenzbooks.com; www.annesspublishing.com

Anness Publishing has a new picture agency outlet for images for publishing, promotions or advertising.
Please visit our website www.practicalpictures.com for more information.

Publisher: Joanna Lorenz
Consultant Editor: Steve Dobell
Project Editor: Joanne Rippin
Designer: Nigel Partridge

PUBLISHER'S NOTE
Although the advice and information in this book are believed to be accurate and true at the time of going to press,
neither the authors nor the publisher can accept any legal responsibility or liability for any
errors or omissions that may have been made.

CONTENTS

CHAPTER ONE

DISCOVERY
AND RAPTURE

Whether love blooms gradually, or hits like a tidal wave, it changes everything. So it was for the young Dante on seeing his Beatrice for the first time, and so it was for Victoria, the enraptured young bride scarcely able to believe her own happiness…

Vita Nuova

I saw her almost at the end of my ninth year. And she appeared to me clothed in a most noble colour, a subdued and decorous crimson; girdled and adorned in such wise as was suitable to her most youthful age... I say that thenceforward Love swayed my soul, which was even then espoused to him; and began to assume over me so great and so assured a lordship, empowered thereto in virtue of my imagination, that I must needs perform to the full all his pleasures. He oftentimes commanded me to seek to behold this youngest Angel; wherefore I in my boyhood many times sought her out, and saw her so noble and laudable in bearing, that certes of her might be spoken that word of the poet Homer: she appeared not to be made by any mortal man, but by God.

DANTE

Sonnet

Shall I compare thee to a summer's day?
Thou art more lovely and more temperate.
Rough winds do shake the darling buds of May,
And summer's lease hath all too short a date.
Sometime too hot the eye of heaven shines,
And often is his gold complexion dimmed;
And every fair from fair sometime declines,
By chance, or nature's changing course,
    untrimmed;
But thy eternal summer shall not fade,
Nor lose possession of that fair thou ow'st,
Nor shall Death brag thou wand'rest in his shade,
When in eternal lines to time thou grow'st.
So long as men can breathe or eyes can see,
So long lives this, and this gives life to thee.

WILLIAM SHAKESPEARE

The Passionate Shepherd to His Love

Come live with me, and be my Love,
And we will all the pleasures prove,
That hills and valleys, dales and fields,
Or woods or steepy mountain yields.

And we will sit upon the rocks,
And see the shepherds feed their flocks
By shallow rivers, to whose falls
Melodious birds sing madrigals.

And I will make thee beds of roses
And a thousand fragrant posies;
A cap of flowers, and a kirtle
Embroidered all with leaves of myrtle.

A gown made of the finest wool
Which from our pretty lambs we pull;
Fair-lined slippers for the cold,
With buckles of the purest gold.

A belt of straw and ivy-buds
With coral clasps and amber studs:
And if these pleasures may thee move,
Come live with me and be my Love.

The shepherd swains shall dance and sing
For thy delight each May morning:
If these delights thy mind may move,
Then live with me and be my Love.

CHRISTOPHER MARLOWE

Sweet is snow in
summer for the thirsty
to drink, and sweet
for sailors after winter
to see the garland of
spring; but most sweet
when one cloak shelters
two lovers, and the tale
of love is told by both.

ASCLEPIADES

Wild Nights – Wild nights!
Were I with thee
Wild Nights should be
Our Luxury!

Futile – the Winds –
To a Heart in port –
Done with the Compass –
Done with the Chart!

Rowing in Eden –
Ah, the Sea!
Might I but Moor – Tonight –
In Thee

EMILY DICKINSON

O You Whom I Often and Silently Come

O You whom I often and silently come where you are that I may be
  with you,
As I walk by your side or sit near, or remain in the same room with you.
Little you know the subtle electric fire that for your sake is playing within me.

WALT WHITMAN

She Walks in Beauty

She walks in beauty, like the night
  Of cloudless climes and starry skies;
And all that's best of dark and bright
  Meet in her aspect and her eyes:
Thus mellowed to that tender light
  Which heaven to gaudy day denies.

One shade the more, one ray the less,
  Had half impaired the nameless grace
Which waves in every raven tress,
  Or softly lightens o'er her face;
Where thoughts serenely sweet express
  How pure, how dear their dwelling-place.

And on that cheek, and o'er that brow,
  So soft, so calm, yet eloquent,
The smiles that win, the tints that glow,
  But tell of days in goodness spent,
A mind at peace with all below,
  A heart whose love is innocent!

LORD BYRON

The woman came toward him holding out her two hands, and ere he could cry out that he knew her, she had thrown herself upon him, and had cast her arms about him and was kissing his face, and murmuring, 'O welcome indeed! welcome, welcome and welcome!' And so sore did his past grief and  his desire move him, that he was weak before her, and held down his hands and let her do. And both those were breathless with wonder and joy and longing; and they stood aloof a little in a while and looked on each other, she with heaving bosom and streaming eyes, and he with arms stretched forth and lips that strove with his heart's words and might not utter them; but once more she gave herself to him, and he took her in his arms strongly now, so that she was frail and weak before him, and he laid his cheek to her cheek and his lips to her lips, and kissed her eyes and her shoulders and murmured over her. And then again they stood apart, and she took him by the hand and led him to the settle, and set him down by her, and herself by him; and for a while they said nought.

WILLIAM MORRIS, THE WATER OF THE WONDROUS ISLES

I will twine the white violet
and I will twine the delicate
narcissus with myrtle buds, and
I will twine laughing lilies, and I
will twine the sweet crocus,
and I will twine therewithal the
crimson hyacinth, and I will
twine lovers' roses, that on
balsam-curled Heliodora's
temples my garland may shed
its petals over the lovelocks of
her hair.

MELEAGER

*M*y love has made me selfish. I cannot exist without you. I am forgetful of everything but seeing you again — my life seems to stop there — I see no further. You have absorbed me. I have a sensation at the present moment as though I was dissolving — I should be exquisitely miserable without the hope of soon seeing you. My sweet Fanny, will your heart never change? My love, will it? I have no limit now to my love… Your note came — it is just here. I cannot be happier away from you. 'Tis richer than an argosy  of Pearles. Do not thwart me even in jest. I have been astonished that men could die Martyrs for religion — I have shuddered at it. I shudder no more — I could be martyred for my religion — Love is my religion. I could die for that. I could die for you.

JOHN KEATS, LETTER TO FANNY BRAWNE

My Little Lize

Who is de prutties' gal you say?
Oh, hush up man an go away.
Yo don't know w'at yo talkin bout;
Yo ought to go an fin' dat out.
De prutties' gal dat one can meet
Dat ever walk along de street;
I guess yo never seen my Lize;
If yo had seen her — bless yo eyes,
Yo would be sure to 'gree wid me,
Dat she's de sweetes' gal dat be.
Why man! where was yo all dis time,
Dat yo don't see dis gal of mine?
Her skin is black an smoode as silk;
Her teet' is jus' as white as milk;
Her hair is of dem fluffy kin',
Wid curls a-hangin, black an shine.
Her shape is such dat can't be beat;
So graceful, slender an so neat.

W'ene'er she turn her eyes on you,
Dey seem to strike yo t'rough an t'rough,
Dere's not a sweeter lookin face;
An lips dat mek yo feel to tas'e.
Her hands is small an so's her feet,
Wid such a pair of enkles neat!
W'en she goes out to tek a walk
She sets de people all to talk.
De gals dey envy her wid fear,
Dey feel so cheap w'en she is near.
De boys dey lif' dere hats an try
To win a smile as she pass by.
But w'at's de use o talkin' so;
An try such beauty here to show!
Yo better see wid yo own eyes
Dis sweet an lovely little Lize;
For if I try de evening t'rough,
I couldn't quite explain to you.

JAMES MARTINEZ

JOURNAL, 12 FEBRUARY 1840

*A*lready the second day since our
marriage; his love and gentleness is
beyond everything, and to kiss that
dear soft cheek, to press my lips to
his, is heavenly bliss. I feel a purer,
more unearthly feeling than I ever did.
Oh! was ever woman so blessed as I am.

QUEEN VICTORIA

O Gongyla, my darling rose,
put on your milk-white gown. I want
you to come back quickly. For my
desire feeds on

your beauty. Each time I see your gown
I am made weak and happy. I too
blamed the Kyprian. Now I pray
she will not seek

revenge, but may she soon allow
you, Gongyla, to come to me
again: you whom of all women
I most desire.

SAPPHO

CHAPTER TWO

LOVES LOST
AND UNREQUITED

Love, alas, does not always last. Sometimes it is not even returned in the first place. The anguish caused by the fading of passion, or by love's sudden loss to a rival or to death, has produced art and literature of almost unbearable sadness...

When You Are Old

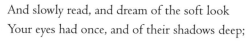

When you are old and grey and full of sleep
And nodding by the fire, take down this book,
>   And slowly read, and dream of the soft look
>   Your eyes had once, and of their shadows deep;

>   How many loved your moments of glad grace,
>   And loved your beauty with love false or true;
>   But one man loved the pilgrim soul in you,
>   And loved the sorrows of your changing face;

>   And bending down beside the glowing bars,
>   Murmur, a little sadly, how love fled
And paced upon the mountains overhead,
And hid his face amid a crowd of stars.

W B YEATS

*T*hat was Dorothea's bent. With all her yearning to know what was afar from her and to be widely benignant, she had ardour enough for what was near, to have kissed Mr Casaubon's coat-sleeve, or to have caressed his shoe-latchet, if he would have made any other sign of acceptance than pronouncing her, with his unfailing propriety, to be of a most affectionate and truly feminine nature, indicating at the same time by politely reaching a chair for her that he regarded these manifestations as rather crude and startling.  Having made his clerical toilette with due care in the morning, he was prepared only for those amenities of life which were suited to the well-adjusted stiff cravat of the period, and to a mind weighted with unpublished matter.

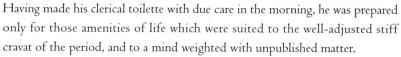

And by a sad contradiction Dorothea's ideas and resolves seemed like melting ice floating and lost in the warm flood of which they had been but another form. She was humiliated to find herself a mere victim of feeling, as if she could know nothing except through that medium: all her strength was scattered in fits of agitation, of struggle, of despondency, and then again in visions of more complete renunciation, transforming all hard conditions into duty. Poor Dorothea! she was certainly troublesome — to herself chiefly; but this morning for the first time she had been troublesome to Mr Casaubon.

GEORGE ELIOT, MIDDLEMARCH

Night

*I*love the silent hour of night,
For blissful dreams may then arise,
Revealing to my charmed sight
What may not bless my waking eyes.

And then a voice may meet my ear,
That death has silenced long ago;
And hope and rapture may appear
Instead of solitude and woe.

Cold in the grave for years has lain
The form it was my bliss to see;
And only dreams can bring again
The darling of my heart to me.

ANNE BRONTË

I got so I could take his name
Without – Tremendous Gain –
that Stop-sensation – on my Soul –
And Thunder – in the Room –

I got so I could walk across
That Angle in the floor,
Where he turned so, and I turned – how –
And all our Sinew tore –

I got so I could stir the Box –
In which his letters grew
Without that forcing, in my breath –
As Staples – driven through –

Could divinely recollect a Grace –
I think, they call it "God" –
Renowned to ease extremity –
When Formula, had failed –

EMILY DICKINSON

So We'll Go No More a Roving

So, we'll go no more a roving
　　So late into the night,
Though the heart be still as loving,
　　And the moon be still as bright.

For the sword outwears its sheath,
　　And the soul wears out the breast,
And the heart must pause to breathe,
　　And love itself have rest.

Though the night was made for loving,
　　And the day returns too soon,
Yet we'll go no more a roving
　　By the light of the moon.

LORD BYRON

33

The Lost Mistress

All's over, then: does truth sound bitter
  As one at first believes?
Hark, 'tis the sparrows' good-night twitter
  About your cottage eaves!

And the leaf-buds on the vine are woolly,
  I noticed that to-day;
One day more bursts them open fully
  —You know the red turns gray.

To-morrow we meet the same then, dearest?
  May I take your hand in mine?
Mere friends are we, — well, friends the merest
  Keep much that I resign:

For each glance of the eye so bright and black,
  Though I keep with heart's endeavour, —
Your voice, when you wish the snowdrops back,
  Though it stay in my soul for ever! —

Yet I will but say what mere friends say,
  Or only a thought stronger;
I will hold your hand but as long as all may,
  Or so very little longer!

ROBERT BROWNING

Paul v. Szinyei 187

Song

My silks and fine array,
  My smiles and languish'd air,
By love are driv'n away;
  And mournful lean Despair
Brings me yew to deck my grave:
Such end true lovers have.

His face is fair as heav'n,
  When springing buds unfold;
O why to him was't giv'n,
  Whose heart is wintry cold?
His breast is love's all worship'd tomb,
Where all love's pilgrims come.

Bring me an axe and spade,
  Bring me a winding sheet;
When I my grave have made,
  Let winds and tempests beat:
Then down I'll lie, as cold as clay.
True love doth pass away!

WILLIAM BLAKE

Kasmiri Song

Pale hands I loved beside the Shalimar,
Where are you now? Who lies beneath your spell?
Whom do you lead on rapture's roadway far,
Before you agonize them in farewell?
Pale hands I loved beside the Shalimar,
Where are you now? Where are you now?

Pale hands, pink tipped, like lotus buds that float
On those cool waters where we used to dwell,
I would have rather felt you round my throat
Crushing out life, than waving me farewell!
Pale hands I loved beside the Shalimar,
Where are you now? Where are you now?

ADELA FLORENCE NICOLSON

37

CHAPTER THREE

LOVE'S STRATAGEMS

The urgent demands of love — and passion — sometimes lead lovers to resort to stratagems of which they ought to be ashamed. Prior's invitation can be seen as cheerful banter and even Marvell's rational entreaty has its sensual humour, but the verbal assault by Laclos's scheming Valmont is positively diabolical...

To Celia

Come, my Celia, let us prove,
While we may, the sports of love;
Time will not be ours, for ever:
He, at length, our good will sever.
Spend not then his gifts in vain.
Suns, that set, may rise again:
But if once we lose this light,
'Tis, with us, perpetual night.
Why should we defer our joys?
Fame and rumour are but toys.
Cannot we delude the eyes
Of a few poor household spies?
Or his easier ears beguile,
So removed by our wile?
'Tis no sin, love's fruit to steal,
But the sweet theft to reveal:
To be taken, to be seen,
These have crimes accounted been.

BEN JONSON

$\mathcal{A}$s stolen love is pleasant to a man, so it is also to a woman; the man dissembles badly; she conceals desire more cleverly.

OVID

$\mathcal{W}$omen are well aware that what is commonly called sublime and poetical love depends not upon moral qualities, but on frequent meetings, and on the style in which the hair is done, and on the colour and cut of the dress.

LEO TOLSTOY, THE KREUTZER SONATA

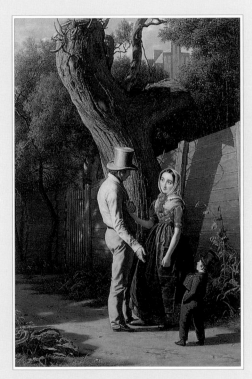

To His Coy Mistress

Had we but world enough, and time,
This coyness, Lady, were no crime.
We would sit down, and think which way
To walk, and pass our long love's day.
Thou by the Indian Ganges' side
Shouldst rubies find: I by the tide
Of Humber would complain. I would
Love you ten years before the flood:
And you should, if you please, refuse
Till the conversion of the Jews.

My vegetable love should grow
Vaster than empires, and more slow.
An hundred years should go to praise
Thine eyes, and on thy forehead gaze.
Two hundred to adore each breast:
But thirty thousand to the rest.
An age at least to every part,
And the last age should show your heart:
For, Lady, you deserve this state;
Nor would I love at lower rate.

But at my back I always hear
Time's wingèd chariot hurrying near:
And yonder all before us lie
Deserts of vast eternity.
Thy beauty shall no more be found;
Nor, in thy marble vault, shall sound
My echoing song: then worms shall try
That long-preserved virginity:

And your quaint honour turn to dust;
And into ashes all my lust.
The grave's a fine and private place,
But none, I think, do there embrace.
   Now, therefore, while the youthful glue
Sits on thy skin like morning dew,
And while thy willing soul transpires
At every pore with instant fires,
Now let us sport us while we may;
And now, like amorous birds of prey,

Rather at once our time devour,
Than languish in his slow-chapped
   power.
Let us roll all our strength, and all
Our sweetness, up into one ball:
And tear our pleasures with rough strife,
Through the iron gates of life.
Thus, though we cannot make our sun
Stand still, yet we will make him run.

ANDREW MARVELL

43

'Adorable woman, you have no idea of the love you inspire; you will never know to what extent you were adored, and how much this sentiment is dearer to me than my existence! May all your days be fortunate and tranquil; may they be embellished by all the happiness of which you have deprived me! At least reward this sincere wish

with a regret, with a tear; and believe that the last of my sacrifices will not be the most difficult for my heart. Farewell.'

While I was speaking, I felt her heart beating violently; I observed the change in her face; I saw above all that she was suffocated by tears but that only a few painful ones flowed. It was at that moment only that I feigned to go away; but, detaining me by force, she said quickly: 'No, listen to me.' 'Let me go,' I answered. 'You will listen to me, I wish it.' 'I must fly from you, I must.' 'No,' she cried. At this last word she rushed or rather fell into my arms in a swoon. As I still doubted of so lucky a success, I feigned a great terror; but with all my terror I guided, or rather, carried her towards the place designed beforehand as the field of my glory; and indeed she only came to her senses submissive and already yielded to her happy conqueror.

CHODERLOS DE LACLOS, LES LIAISONS DANGEREUSES

Since we your husband daily see
    So jealous out of season;
Phillis, let you and I agree,
    To make him so with reason.

I'm vext to think that every night,
    A sot within thy arms,
Tasting the most divine delight,
    Should sully all your charms.

While fretting I must lie alone,
    Cursing the powers divine;
That undeservedly have thrown
    A Pearl unto a Swine.

Then, Phillis, heal my wounded heart,
    My burning passion cool;
Let me at least in thee have part,
    With thy insipid fool.

Let him, by night, his joys pursue,
    And blunder in the dark;
While I, by day, enjoying you,
    Can see to hit the mark.

MATTHEW PRIOR

La Belle Dame Sans Merci

O what can ail thee, Knight at arms,
    Alone and palely loitering?
The sedge has withered from the Lake,
    And no birds sing! …

I met a Lady in the Meads
    Full beautiful – a faery's child;
Her hair was long, her foot was light,
    And her eyes were wild –

I made a garland for her head,
    And bracelets too, and fragrant zone;
She looked at me as she did love,
    And made sweet moan. …

She took me to her elfin grot
    And there she wept and sighed full sore;
And there I shut her wild wild eyes
    With kisses four.

And there she lulled me asleep,
    And there I dreamed – Ah! woe betide!
The latest dream I ever dreamt,
    On the cold hill's side.

I saw pale Kings, and Princes too,
    Pale warriors – death pale were they all;
They cried, 'La belle dame sans merci
    Hath thee in thrall!'

I saw their starved lips in the gloam,
    With horrid warning gaped wide;
And I awoke, and found me here
    On the cold hill's side.

And this is why I sojourn here,
    Alone and palely loitering;
Though the sedge is withered from the Lake,
    And no birds sing.

JOHN KEATS

CHAPTER FOUR

UNDYING LOVE

True love overcomes many obstacles. The refusal by faithful lovers to allow distance, disapproval, or even death to affect their feelings can sometimes seem like fanaticism or obsession, but in the very stubborness of the declarations of undying love there is consolation, satisfaction and immense beauty...

Danny Boy

Oh, Danny boy, the pipes, the pipes are calling
From glen to glen, and down the mountain side.
The summer's gone and all the roses falling,
It's you, it's you must go and I must bide.
But come ye back when summer's in the meadow,
Or when the valley's hushed and white with
   snow,
It's I'll be here in sunshine or in shadow,
Oh, Danny boy, oh, Danny boy, I love you so!

But when ye come, and all the flowers are dying,
If I am dead, as dead I well may be,
Ye'll come and find the place where I am lying,
And kneel and say an Ave there for me.
And I shall hear, though soft you tread above me,
And all my grave will warmer, sweeter be,
For you will bend and tell me that you love me,
And I shall sleep in peace until you come to me!

FRED E WEATHERLY

*T*he bowers whereat, in dreams, I see
The wantonest singing birds,
Are lips – and all thy melody
If lip-begotten words –

Thine eyes, in heaven of heart enshrined
Then desolately fall,
O God! on my funereal mind
Like starlight on a pall –

Thy heart – *thy* heart! I wake and sigh,
and sleep to dream till day
Of truth that love can never buy –
Of the baubles that it may.

EDGAR ALLEN POE

Remember

Remember me when I am gone away,
   Gone far away into the silent land;
   When you can no more hold me by the hand,
Nor I half turn to go yet turning stay.
Remember me when no more day by day
   You tell me of our future that you planned:
   Only remember me; you understand …

It will be late to counsel then or pray.
Yet if you should forget me for a while
   And afterwards remember, do not grieve:
   For if the darkness and corruption leave
   A vestige of the thoughts that once I had,
Better by far you should forget and smile
   Than that you should remember and be sad.

CHRISTINA ROSSETTI

*A*nd Ruth said, 'Intreat me not to leave thee, or to return from following after thee: for whither thou goest, I will go; and where thou lodgest, I will lodge: thy people shall be my people, and thy God my God: where thou diest, will I die, and there will I be buried: the Lord do so to me, and more also, if ought but death part thee and me.

THE BOOK OF RUTH

Annabel Lee

*I*t was many and many a year ago,
   In a kingdom by the sea,
That a maiden there lived whom you may know
   By the name of Annabel Lee; –
And this maiden she lived with no other thought
   Than to love and be loved by me.

She was a child and *I* was a child,
   In this kingdom by the sea,
But we loved with a love that was more than love –
   I and my Annabel Lee –
With a love that the wingèd seraphs of Heaven
   Coveted her and me.

And this was the reason that, long ago,
    In this kingdom by the sea,
A wind blew out of a cloud by night
    Chilling my Annabel Lee;
So that her highborn kinsmen came
    And bore her away from me,
To shut her up in a sepulchre
    In this kingdom by the sea.

The angels, not half so happy in Heaven,
    Went envying her and me: —
Yes! that was the reason (as all men know,
    In this kingdom by the sea)
That the wind came out of a cloud, chilling
    And killing my Annabel Lee.

But our love it was stronger by far than the love
    Of those who were older than we —
    Of many far wiser than we —
And neither the angels in Heaven above
    Nor the demons down under the sea,
Can ever dissever my soul from the soul
    Of the beautiful Annabel Lee: —

For the moon never beams without bringing me
        dreams
    Of the beautiful Annabel Lee;
And the stars never rise but I see the bright eyes
    Of the beautiful Annabel Lee;
And so, all the night-tide, I lie down by the side
Of my darling, my darling, my life and my bride,
    In her sepulchre there by the sea —
    In her tomb by the sounding sea.

                              EDGAR ALLEN POE

57

Portuguese Sonnet

How do I love thee: Let me count the ways.
I love thee to the depth and breadth and height
My soul can reach, when feeling out of sight
For the ends of Being and ideal Grace.
I love to the level of every day's
Most quiet need, by sun and candlelight.
I love thee freely, as men strive for Right;
I love thee purely, as they turn from Praise.
I love thee with the passion put to use
In my old griefs, and with my childhood's faith.
I love thee with a love I seemed to lose
With my lost saints, — I love thee with the breath,
Smiles, tears, of all my life! — and, if God choose,
I shall but love thee better after death.

ELIZABETH BARRETT BROWNING

In Memorium

Dark house, by which once more I stand
   Here in the long unlovely street,
   Doors, where my heart was used to beat
So quickly, waiting for a hand,

A hand that can be clasp'd no more —
   Behold me, for I cannot sleep,
   And like a guilty thing I creep
At earliest morning to the door.

He is not here; but far away
   The noise of life begins again,
   And ghastly through the drizzling rain
On the bald street breaks the blank day.

                ALFRED, LORD TENNYSON

"You teach me now how cruel you've been — cruel and false. *Why* did you despise me? *Why* did you betray your own heart, Cathy? I have not one word of comfort — you deserve this. You have killed yourself. Yes, you may kiss me, and cry; and wring out my kisses and tears. They'll blight you — they'll damn you. You loved me — then what *right* had you to leave me? What right — answer me — for the poor fancy you felt for Linton? Because misery, and degradation, and death, and nothing that God or satan could inflict would have parted us, *you*, of your own will, did it. I have not broken your heart — *you* have broken it — and in breaking it, you have broken mine. So much the worse for me, that I am strong. Do I want to live? What kind of living will it be when you — oh, God! would *you* like to live with your soul in the grave?

EMILY BRONTË, *WUTHERING HEIGHTS*

Non Sum Qualis Eram Bonae Sub Regno Cynarae

Last night, ah, yesternight, betwixt her lips and mine
There fell thy shadow, Cynara! thy breath was shed
Upon my soul between the kisses and the wine;
And I was desolate and sick of an old passion,
    Yea, I was desolate and bowed my head:
I have been faithful to thee, Cynara! in my fashion.

All night upon my heart I felt her warm heart beat,
Night-long within mine arms in love and sleep she lay;
Surely the kisses of her bought red mouth were sweet;
But I was desolate and sick of an old passion,
    When I awoke and found the dawn was grey:
I have been faithful to thee, Cynara! in my fashion.

I have forgot much, Cynara! gone with the wind,
Flung roses, roses riotously with the throng,
Dancing, to put thy pale, lost lilies out of mind;
But I was desolate and sick of an old passion,
    Yea, all the time, because the dance was long:
I have been faithful to thee, Cynara! in my fashion.

ERNEST DOWSON

Acknowledgements

The following pictures are reproduced with kind permission of
The Visual Arts Library, London:
Front jacket: Couple in Love c1850 by Sremradzki, Ljwow Museum, Ukraine/Edimedia. Back jacket: (see p22) Romeo and Juliet,1884 by Frank Dicksee, Southampton Art Gallery. p2: Louis XV declaring himself to Madame du Barry, 1877 by Joseph Caraud, Carcassonne, Musee des Beaux-Arts/Edimedia. p7: Romeo and Juliet, 1884 by Frank Dicksee, Southampton Art Gallery. p8: Noonday Rest by JW Godward, 1910, private collection. p9: The Companion, 1889 by BE Ward, private collection. p11: The Hireling Shepherd (detail) by Holman Hunt, Walker Art Gallery, Liverpool/Edimedia. p12: A Young Couple in the Country by J-B Huet, private collection/Edimedia. p15: Angelica Catalani, 1806 by E Vigee-Lebrun, Kimbell Art Museum. p18: A Summer Offering, 1894, private collection. p19: The Pensive Violinist, 1861 by O Scholderer, Frankfurt Kunstinstitut. p23: In the Rose Garden by Alma-Tadema, 1889, private collection/Edimedia. p25: The Lady of Shalot by JW Waterhouse, 1888, Tate Gallery. p26: Beata Krans by O Krans, c1900, Historical Society, Chicago. p27: Maida in our Paris Studio by Pitts, 19th cent, Detroit Institute of Art. p28: A Couple by F Ittenbach (attrib) c1830, Musee du Louvre, Paris. p30: A Woman Closing her Eyes by EV Prouve, 1905, Petit-Palais, Paris. p32/3: A Couple in Love by H Siemiradszki, 19th cent, Ljwow Museum, Ukraine/Edimedia. p36: A Woman Asleep by L Lagrenee, 1773, Clermont-Ferrand, Musee des Beaux-Arts. p37 The Hareem's Favourites by Manovens, 1881, private collection/Edimedia. p39 The Scorceress by JW Waterhouse, 1901, private collection/Edimedia. p40: Courting by A Perez, private collection/Edimedia. p41: The Proposal by D Monies, 19th cent, private collection/Edimedia. p42: The Young Couple by M Moreels, private collection/Edimedia. p44: Jealousy by H Fuseli, 1819-25, O Reinhart Foundation, Winterthur. p46: Rolla by H Gervex, 1878, Musee des Beaux-Arts, Bordeaux/Edimedia. p49: La Belle Dame sans Merci by JW Waterhouse, Darmstadt, Hessiches Landesmuseum/Edimedia. p51: Lovers under a Blossom Tree by J Horsely, 1895, Philadelphia Museum of Art. p53: Study for Vanity by JW Waterhouse, private collection/Edimedia. p54: The Convalescent by JJ Tissot c1895, Sheffield Art Gallery. p56: Ask me no More by Alma-Tadema, 1886, private collection. p58: Young Man Dreaming by H Ededius, 1895, National Museum, Oslo. p58: The Betrothal by OT Leyde, Musee des Beaux-Arts, Strasbourg/Edimedia.

The Bridgeman Art Library, London:
p13: Romeo and Juliet by John Francis Rigaud, Agnew & Sons, London. p14: Nordic Summer Evening, 1899–1900 by Sven Richard Bergh, Goteborgs Konstmuseum, Sweden. p17: The Betrothal of Robert Burns and Highland Mary by James Archer, Forbes Magazine Collection, London. p21: Portrait of a Negress by Marie Guilhelmine Benoist, Louvre, Paris/Giraudon. p22: The Honeymoon by Robert Hannah, Rafael Valls Gallery. p29: The Day Before the Marriage by George Baxter, Maidstone Museum and Art Gallery, Kent. p31: Negress with a Cloche Hat by Emile Bernard, Connaught Brown, London. p34 From the Miller's Daughter by Tennyson by JA Vintner, Wolverhampton Art Gallery, Staffs. p35: The Lovers by Pal Szinyel Merse, Magyar Nemzeti Galeria, Budapest. p43: The Stolen Kiss c1788 by Jean-Honore Fragonard, Hermitage, St Petersburg. p45: The Bolt by Jean-Honore Fragonard, Louvre, Paris. p52: Mated by Marcus Stone, York City Art Gallery. p55: Hesperus by Sir Joseph Noel Paton, Glasgow Art Gallery & Museum. p57: Naked Young Man Sitting by the Sea, 1836 by Hippolyte Flandrin, Louvre, Paris. p61: The Confession by Sir Frank Dicksee, Roy Miles Gallery, 29 Bruton Street, London. p62/3 Naked Lady from Behind by Jean-Auguste Dominique Ingres, Musee Bonnat, Bayonne.